D1825225

# GETTING THROUGH THE DIFFICULT TIMES IN LIFE

*Daily Reflections*

JEWEL HARPER MPA, MDIV

WESTBOW
PRESS®
A DIVISION OF THOMAS NELSON
& ZONDERVAN

WestBow Press books may be ordered through booksellers or by contacting:

WestBow Press
A Division of Thomas Nelson & Zondervan
1663 Liberty Drive
Bloomington, IN 47403
www.westbowpress.com
844-714-3454

ISBN: 978-1-6642-2948-8 (sc)
ISBN: 978-1-6642-2950-1 (hc)
ISBN: 978-1-6642-2949-5 (e)

Library of Congress Control Number: 2021906436

Print information available on the last page.

WestBow Press rev. date: 5/12/2021

# INTRODUCTION

*Getting through the Difficult Times in Life* is the result of my journaling. It is through God's love and direction that he directs my path in life and gives me purpose and mission. Many prayers and tears have been shed, loss of family and friends during the Coronavirus. This daily reflection have helped me to grow and change. God's change me and gave me meaning and purpose for getting me through difficult times in my life. I have been able to create these daily reflections for those who want to grow, change, and develop deeper spirituality.

While the coronavirus has been a part of my isolation time, I've had the opportunity to add on to some of the reflections and develop them further. After my first daily reflection book, *Footsteps to Christ*, I continued with my journaling and developed this book, which offers a wide variety of meditation topics about real-life events that deal with difficult time. It is through the difficult times that I have been transformed into a new person.

This book is meant for those who are sixteen and older. It is for those at all stages of their spiritual development and is continuing their journey in life. A wide variety of experiences with views, concepts, and issues have been provided. I hope the topics will help everyone find what he or she needs.

Use this book as a part of your daily devotional exercise. I have included a topic index at the back of the book; you can focus your meditation on the subjects with a Bible study.

*Getting through the Difficult Times in Life* will inspire you as it has inspired me. I am grateful to have had the opportunity to be a part of this project. I hope this book proves useful to you and your groups in providing the strength needed to not give up and not give in to life's struggles. Thank you for allowing me to be a part of your journey today.

This book is dedicated to those who have and are currently experiencing difficult times in their lives.

To my close family and friends who are such a great inspiration – Thank you Dr. Ramona Joseph D. Min

# TRANSFORMATION

Show me your ways, Lord, teach me your paths. Guide me in your truth and teach me, for you are God my Savior, and my hope is in you all day long. (Psalm 25:4–5)

Transformation is a change in thinking, behavior, and lifestyle. At the start of my spiritual journey, I started making changes slowly. I had to let go of things that hindered my spiritual journey such as various temptations and undue attachments that tried to keep me from growing in Christ.

Transformation is all about change, growth, and development. It requires us to study the Bible. It allows the Word to be a practical application in our lives. Now that I have allowed God to enter my life, I have begun to learn what His purpose and plan is for me. I have been strengthened and transformed in having a passion for servanthood. Paul wrote that being transformed into the image of Christlikeness was a process; it takes time and is a constant struggle over temptations. One of the problems with transforming my life is learning to resist temptations and surrender to Christ.

Allowing Christ to transform me required me to allow Christ to be my mentor. Daily changes like exploring the Bible, helping others, witnessing, and sharing my experiences will make me more attentive to moving toward the likeness of Christ every day. I have no restraints that hold me back from loving and serving the Lord. My self-care includes prayer, daily meditation, reading the Bible, and taking time for prayer retreats and self-help writings.

### *Prayer*

Lord, I desire to imitate you, to journey with you as my transformation from my past to my present begins. With my journey, I can follow the footprints that leave impressions for me and others to follow. I place all my trust and faith in you. Keep me focused, and help me during times of weakness to resist temptations and reach for your strength so I will follow your path. Thank you for allowing me to speak, listen, serve, and love you and others through this journey as I follow you.

# TRANSFORMING INTO CHRISTLIKENESS

> And we all, who with unveil faces contemplate the Lord's glory, are being transformed into his image with ever increasing glory, which comes from the Lord, who is the Spirit. (2 Corinthians 3:18)

I love looking at the many varieties of butterflies. In understanding beauty, I first had to understand its process. A caterpillar is born with the life that causes it to transform into a butterfly. It does not put on a mask or strive to act differently from when it was in a cocoon. As it eats, its metabolism assimilates the nutrients it consumes into a caterpillar and causes it to grow so that eventually, the caterpillar becomes a butterfly. This is a picture of what the Bible speaks of concerning the transforming of the believers into the likeness of Christ. The Bible speaks of the goal of the Christian life in 2 Corinthians 3:18: "We are being transformed into Christ's likeness," while Romans 8:29 states that God "predestined all believers to be conformed to the image of his Son. The image of Christ is God's goal for all who trust in Christ, and that is my goal also." The words *transformed* and *conformed* have a common root—a pattern or a mold. Being transformed refers to the process; conformed refers to the finished product. Jesus is my pattern or mold. I am being transformed so that I will eventually be conformed to the likeness of Christ.

## Prayer

Lord, mold me for I am open for change. Help me in my transformation so that in my journey in life, I will conform to your likeness.

# STUDYING THE WORD

All Scripture is God-breathed and is useful for teaching, rebuking, correcting, and training in righteousness, So that the servant of God may be thoroughly equipped for every good work. (2 Timothy 3:16–17)

The Bible is the Word of God. It contains the mind of God and His will for us. That is why the Bible was given to us. Every word of God is pure; He is a shield for those who trust Him.

Knowing the will of God is important especially when I am praying. Some of my unanswered prayers are a result of my not knowing God's will. The Bible is so clear in 1 John 5:14: "This is the confidence we have in approaching God; that if we ask anything according to his will, he hears us." This promise that the Lord has given us is answered with a condition attached to it: if we ask according to His will only.

The Bible is the only book in which God has revealed His will to us. In knowing His will for our lives, my prayer will be changed from asking Him to protect me from harm and danger to declaring that I will never be harmed or be faced with danger again. It is by testing my discernment and asking questions about what the will of God is, what is good and acceptable and perfect, that He has revealed His will for my life. In studying the Word, I was amazed at what I learned about His will.

### *Prayer*

Lord, I am grateful for your insight into your will and teaching me how to pray. Open my mind and continue to give me a willingness to learn, grow from your word and equipping me daily to be your humble servant.

# HAVING A RENEWED MIND

Do not conform to the pattern of this world but be transformed by the renewing of your mind. Then you will be able to test and approve what God's will is—his good, pleasing, and perfect will. (Romans 12:2)

I can renew my mind by studying the Word of God; it has changed my thinking, my behavior, and my lifestyle. I once met a tour guide in Colorado who told me that he had had an addiction in high school—his parents' prescription pills. Several times a day, he thought about taking the pills. He was unable to sleep until he thought about how he could get more pills without being caught.

He shared that for a few years lately, he had been with the Lord because of his youth pastor. He was in recovery when I met him, and he said that the Word sanctified his mind and that the more he studied it, the more his head got straight. John 17:17 can be paraphrase to mean here to sanctify us by the truth; God's Word is truth.

## *Prayer*

Lord, I am so grateful for the renewed mind. Changing my thinking, behavior, and lifestyle brings about new beginnings daily.

# THE WORD OF GOD HELPS US GET THROUGH THE DIFFICULT TIMES IN LIFE

The grass withers, the flowers fall, but the word of our God endures forever. (Isaiah 40:8)

Your word is a lamp for my feet, a light on my path. (Psalm 119:105)

So do not fear, for I am with you; do not be dismayed, for I am your God, I will strengthen you and help you; I will uphold you with my righteous right hand. (Isaiah 41:10)

About thirty years ago, my family went through the darkest days of our lives. Something bad happened that left every member of my family distressed and sad. It was the first time I experienced such trauma in my life. My whole body felt so weak. I was not sick physically; I felt sick in my heart, and I could not find the strength to pull myself together. I would look at my Bible lying on the table, but I could not pick it up and read it.

During this time, I learned something important—the Word gives us strength during difficult times, but I could not read my Bible because of the anger and sadness I was experiencing.

The Word of God came to me while I was reflecting on some of the promises God was revealing in my mind while giving me strength. My friends and extended family along with my prayer group supported me in prayer with inspirational passages from the Bible. God's Word gave me strength in times of trouble when I did not have the strength to pull the Bible from the table. During my weakness, the Word of God provided me the strength I needed to get through one day at a time.

## *Prayer*

Thank you for the strength that you continue to provide during my difficult times in life. Lord, you continue to send positive and encouraging people to provide support.

# THE WORD OF GOD IS
# TOTALLY AUTHORITATIVE

> In the beginning was the Word, and the Word was with God, and the Word was God. He was with God in the beginning. Through him all things were made; without him nothing was made that has been made. (John 1:1–3)

> For the word of God is alive and active. Sharper than any double-edged sword, it penetrates even to dividing soul and spirit, joints, and marrow; it judges the thoughts and attitude of the heart. (Hebrews 4:12)

The Word of God is the only source of absolute divine authority. This divine authority is meant for me as a servant of Jesus Christ. When someone said to me, "I have a word from the Lord for you," I wrote it down and studied God's Word to see if the Lord was speaking to me through His scriptures and that person.

It is important for Christians to be secure and trust in the Lord. They should not be easily misled; by studying the Bible, they are able to obey God's Word and allow Him to guide and direct their lives in the plan He has for them.

## *Prayer*

Lord, in learning more about you and building my relationship with you, how excited I am as your servant to serve you. Your Word continues to be a source for absolute divine authority in my life.

# THE WORD OF GOD WILL ACCOMPLISH WHAT IT PROMISES

> So is my word that goes out from my mouth: It will not return to me empty but will accomplish what I desire and achieve the purpose for which I sent it. (Isaiah. 55:11)

> Do not conform to the pattern of this world but be transformed by the renewing of your mind. Then you will be able to test and approve what God's will is—his good, pleasing, and perfect will. (Romans 12:2)

God sent His Word to accomplish His perfect will for my life. If God makes a promise to me, He will fulfill it in His own time. There are so many promises given to us in the Bible. These promises have reassured and comforted me during my crises and trials.

My challenge is to take time to study the Word of God. The Lord has shown me how wonderful things will change in my life. God eased my life as He promised "while crying out to him and he answered me! He freed me from all my fears" as summed up in Psalm 34:1–7.

God is greater than anything that can harm me. I know God will deliver me from trouble even if it's all the way to glory. I have no fear today or tomorrow because God has my back, and He holds me.

## Prayer

Lord you have a purpose and plan for my life. My trials have been lessons revealed that have shown wonderful things that have changed my life.

# HAVING A SERVANT ATTITUDE

For even the Son of Man did not come to be served, but to
serve, and to give his life as a ransom for many. (Mark 10:45)

A true act of service is when I feel heartfelt and motivated to do something alone. One reason for doing service projects is to share the love of Christ with those who do not have a relationship with Him. This is pretty much the main reason people go on mission trips with churches and organizations.

How can I serve? I can serve by cleaning a house or church, mowing the grass, helping a friend out with homework, being kind to someone new at school or someone who is being bullied at school, unloading the dishwasher at home, or buying someone's lunch or dinner for them. I can serve others by praying! The list could go on and on about how I could serve others.

When can I serve others? I can serve others anytime of the day, week, and month. I can serve my parents by visiting them. I can serve whenever I am at school, church, and even at my friend's house. There are numerous opportunities to serve throughout every day.

What does true service look like? God instructs me to serve others. Paraphrasing Galatians 5:13–14, "You, my brother, and sisters, were called to be free. But do not use your freedom to indulge the flesh; rather, serve one another humbly in love. For the entire law is fulfilled in keeping this one command, 'Love your neighbor as yourself.'"

This passage is talking about how I should serve others rather than myself. The definition of service is love in action. This helpful action referred to in this definition implies that when I am doing various tasks while helping others on my own time, I also share the love of Christ with those I am serving. I should also have a clean and humble heart while serving because it is not for my glory but for God's glory. Service is not to make me feel good but to help others who are going through difficult times or just need help with various tasks.

The Bible has a lot to say about servanthood because the central theme of the Bible is the Servant as Jesus Christ. When I give Jesus Christ His rightful place as Lord of my life, His lordship is expressed in the way I serve others as identified in Mark 9:35, 1 Peter 4:10, and John 15:12–13.

My love for God is expressed in my love for others. "For what I preach is not for myself, but Jesus Christ as Lord, and myself as your servants for Jesus sake" (2 Corinthians 4:5).

## Prayer

To you my Lord, as your servant, help me to keep my mind clean in having a servant's heart. Teach me more about loving and serving others and help me demonstrate love for you as your servant.

# LEARNING TO BE A SERVANT

Who, being in very nature God, did not consider equality with God something to be used to his own advantage? (Philippians 2:6)

Rather, he made himself nothing by taking the very nature of a servant, being made in human likeness. (Philippians 2:7)

Servant leaders seek the glory of their leader. I am called to lead as a servant. I am called to humility.

The people I serve are not called to serve my agenda, and I am called to serve only God's agenda for their lives. Christlike leaders are bondservants of Christ (Ephesians 6:6), and they demonstrate over time that Christ—not public approval, position, or financial security—is their primary loyalty.

God does not need middle management as He has all the management He needs by the power and revelation of His Holy Spirit on earth. I must get out of His way and serve only in His way. Jesus said, "The one who speaks on his own authority seeks his own glory; but the one who seeks the glory of him who sent him is true, and in him there is no falsehood" (John 7:18).

## *Prayer*

Lord, help me to get out of your way and do your will. Servanthood requires me to lead as a servant and surrender all of me to you.

# SERVANT LEADERS SACRIFICIALLY SEEK THE HIGHEST JOY OF THOSE THEY SERVE

Not so with you. Instead, whoever wants to become great among you must be your servant. (Matthew 20:26)

Just as the Son of Man did not come to be served, but to serve, and to give his life as a ransom for many. (Matthew 20:28)

A servant leader would rather lose his rights rather than deny the gospel. "A servant leader's identity and trust are not in his calling, but in his Christ." As Paul said, "I have made myself a servant to all, that I might win more of them" (1 Corinthians 9:19). It implied that sometimes Paul abstained from certain foods and drinks, and Paul refused financial support from those he served, he worked with his hands to provide for himself, went hungry or dressed poorly, was beaten or was homeless, and endured disrespect inside and outside the church (1 Corinthians 4:11–13, 9:4–7). And he decided not to marry (1 Corinthians 9:5). All this was before he was martyred. As a servant, Paul yielded his rights with the belief that more would be won to Christ as a result.

As a servant leader, I try not to be preoccupied with personal visibility and recognition. Like John the Baptist, servant leaders saw himself as "friend of the Bridegroom"(John 3:29) and was not preoccupied with the visibility of roles. He did not view those with less as less significant, nor did he view the visible roles as more significant (Corinthians 12:12-26). His ministry sought to steward the roles he received as best he could and gladly left the assigning of roles to God (John 3:27).

As a servant leader, I must first see myself with the natural feeling of wanting to serve—to serve first. Then, my conscious choice will bring me to aspire to lead. I am different from that person who is a leader first. The leader first and the servant first are two extreme types. Between, them are blends of the infinite variety of human nature.

The difference manifests itself in the care taken by the servant first to make sure that those with high-priority needs are being served. Do I who served grow as a person? Do those while being served become healthier, wiser, freer, more autonomous, and more likely to become servants?

A servant leader focuses primarily on the growth and well-being of people and their communities. Servant leaders share power, put the needs of others first, and help people develop and perform as best they can.

This paraphrased passage connotes that servant leaders anticipate and graciously accept the time for their decrease. All leaders serve only for a season. Some seasons are long, some short; some are abundant, some lean; some are recorded and recalled; most are not. But all seasons end. When John the Baptist recognized the ending of his season, he said, "Therefore this joy of mine is now complete. He must increase, but I must decrease" (John 3:29–30).

Sometimes, leaders are the first to recognize their seasons' ends; sometimes, others recognize it first; and sometimes, God lets a season end unjustly for purposes a leader cannot understand at the time. Servant leaders graciously yield their roles for the good of Christ's because their identity and trust are not in their calling but in Christ's.

True leadership is servanthood, and the greatest leader of all is Jesus Christ. Servanthood is an attitude exemplified by Christ; the five words in the New Testament translated generally refer to servanthood or service given in love. Serving others is the very essence of ministry. All believers are called to ministry summarizing Matthew 28:18–20, and therefore, we are all called to be servants for the glory of God. Living is giving; all else is selfishness and boredom.

## *Prayer*

Lord, thank you for the opportunities to give love by serving your people. When my time has ended, direct my path to a new season so I may see the rich seeds that have been sowed as your servant. I Love your people with the attitude of servanthood exemplified by you as my example. Amen.

# TRAINING FOR CHANGE

> I went down to the potter's house, and I saw him working
> at the wheel. But the pot he was shaping from the clay was
> marred in his hands; so, the potter formed it into another
> pot, shaping it as seemed best to him. Then the word of the
> LORD came to me. He said, "Can I not do with you, Israel,
> as this potter does?" declares the LORD. "Like clay in the
> hand of the potter, so are you in my hand, Israel." (Jeremiah
> 18:3–6)

Jeremiah 18 says that God is the Potter and we are the clay. It is up to God to mold, transform, and sanctify us as we journey through this earthly life. God makes promises to us and fulfills them in His time. There are so many promises given to us that are found in the Bible. These promises have reassured me and brought me comfort in times of trials.

I challenge you to take the time to study the Word of God. The Lord has shown me wonderful things that have changed my life.

The Potter continues to make changes with the clay. I live in times of change. Change is everywhere around us. It always was and always will be. My life, the whole universe, exists through continuous change. I know this because I experience it every day. No day is the same. Our bodies change nonstop. The weather is always changing. Plants, trees, rocks, rivers, and seas change. Our relationships, friends, colleagues, customers, suppliers, and others change. I live through change every day, and I am extremely capable of dealing with it.

I find two kinds of leaders: those who lead change as a continuous learning experience, and those who do not.

## Prayer

Lord, change me and allow me to surrender my will. Remove the fear and the desire to control situations, events, and people. Supply me with compassion, hope and peace as I surrender to your will daily.

# BEING OPEN-MINDED

Then he opened their minds so they could understand the
Scriptures. (Luke 24:45)

It's not always easy to be open-minded. Growing up, I learned a certain set of
values and beliefs. Due to time, travel, and people I met, I began to develop a
set of values and beliefs with which I was able to change my thinking about
life. So when others present me with a viewpoint or perspective different from
mine, I can now be open to thinking about their ideas. It was difficult for me
to be open, but I had to put my ego aside and ask myself, *What can I learn from*
*that person's opinion? Can I apply it to my life in some way and continue to be open*
*to change my own thoughts?*

We can gain quite a bit by opening the door to our minds. I know plenty
of people who used to be rigid in their thoughts and beliefs but who over the
years loosened up, let go, and became more open-minded. They tend to carry
less stress now and more peace and contentment.

### *Prayer*

Lord, help me not have a close mind and be judgmental. Teach me to have an
open mind to learn from others and grow in your Word. It is through change in
my lifestyle that I can continue on my journey and to achieve the purpose and
plan that you have for me.

# LEARNING FROM SPIRITUAL LEADERS

As Jesus was walking beside the Sea of Galilee, he saw two brothers, Simon called Peter and his brother Andrew. They were casting a net into the lake, for they were fishermen. "Come, follow me," Jesus said, "and I will send you out to fish for people." At once they left their nets and followed him. Going on from there, he saw two other brothers, James son of Zebedee and his brother John. They were in a boat with their father Zebedee, preparing their nets. Jesus called them, mediately they left the boat and their father and followed him. (Matthew 4:18–22)

Our Lord Jesus Christ was the perfect example of mentoring. He taught His disciples to follow Him and model Him by living with them (John 1:38–39). He asked the disciples to put away their current occupations to walk alongside Him and learn from Him (Matthew 4:18–22).

The apostle Paul said that his followers should look to him as an example in the same way he looked to Christ (1 Corinthians 11:1). This was a simple principle of spiritual mentorship. All students need examples to follow, and their teachers need to be the best they can be (2 Thessalonians 3:9). This does not mean that teachers will never make mistakes; it means that teachers should strive to be good examples.

## *Prayer*

Lord, you are my perfect example for instruction and learning. Bring in that special person who will teach me by example so I may strive to be the best person I can be.

# SOMEONE WHO BELIEVES IN YOU

> Sometime later Paul said to Barnabas, "Let us go back and visit the believers in all the towns where we preached the word of the Lord and see how they are doing." Barnabas wanted to take John, also called Mark, with them, but Paul did not think it wise to take him, because he had deserted them in Pamphylia and had not continued with them in the work. They had such a sharp disagreement that they parted company. Barnabas took Mark and sailed for Cyprus, but Paul chose Silas and left, commended by the believers to the grace of the Lord. He went through Syria and Cilicia, strengthening the churches. (Acts 15:36–41)

Everyone desires affirmation. My mentor is someone who believes in me even when I do not understand the clutter and imperfections in my life. My mentor will listen carefully to my passions, dreams, goals, hang-ups, and immature ideas. Mentors provide caring; they are objective and trustworthy, and they consider their sense of how God is working in my life. This is paraphrased in Barnabas and John Mark (Acts 15:36–39; 2 Timothy 4:11).

## *Prayer*

Lord, bring in that special someone into my life to believe in me. Allow me to be open so I may begin to dream dreams and follow your purpose that you have in my life.

# A ROLE MODEL

Follow my example, as I follow the example of Christ.
(1 Corinthians 11:1)

Mentors have a tall order to fill by presenting themselves as role models in their walk as well as in talk. Spiritually, this means that they lead with their lives. God has commanded by the scripture that role models lead by the Holy Spirit and present themselves as godly role models of Christlike behavior to those they mentor.

## *Prayer*

Lord, Teach me to be open in making right choices. Allow me to present myself as a godly role model of Christlikeness.

# PROMOTING SPIRITUAL GROWTH

> Brothers and sisters, I do not consider myself yet to have taken hold of it. But one thing I do: Forgetting what is behind and straining toward what is ahead. (Philippians 3:13)

My spiritual mentors have helped me develop a solid pattern of spiritual discipline. They have helped deepen my personal relationship with God and have helped me grow in the image of Christ, and they have prepared me to become most usable for the kingdom.

These spiritual activities include formal and informal Bible study, directed reading, training in the Christian disciplines (quiet time, Bible reading, prayer, etc.), and determining spiritual gifts and ministry direction. The spiritual life patterns established early in my relationships are designed to benefit me for a lifetime (Philippians 3:13).

### *Prayer*

Lord, I need to transform my life with discipline. Help me to not give up or give in. Help me to deepen my relationship with you, and help those I encounter.

# ACCOUNTABILITY

Rooted and built up in him, strengthened in the faith as you were taught, and overflowing with thankfulness. (Colossians 2:7)

The world has many obstacles and diversions—the coronavirus, loss of family members, social-injustice movements, and more. It is easy for temptations to attempt to derail my earnest desire of deepening my relationship with God. Therefore, having a mentor who is my accountability partner is an invaluable benefit for asking tough questions, heading off danger, and derailing diversions. I need to change my behavior and practice a positive attitude of gratitude.

## *Prayer*

Today, I felt weak, and I had to spend some quiet time with you. I saw some landmines and diversions that tried to get my attention, but I asked you for help and strength during this difficult time. You sent positive and encouraging people into my life to help me. Thank you for being number one in my life and sending people who love and encourage me.

# BE AN ENCOURAGER

> Joseph, a Levite from Cyprus, whom the apostles called Barnabas (which means "son of encouragement"), sold a field he owned and brought the money and put it at the apostles' feet. (Acts 4:36–37)

While the Bible is clear that we should look out for the needs of others, we often fail to follow through. Servants benefit from proactive encouragement from leaders who understand the power and value of another encourager (Acts 4:36–37, 9:26–30, 11:22–30).

## *Prayer*

Lord, life's problems make it difficult to be an encourager. Too much childhood trauma can continue into adult life. Hurt people hurt others. Learning to look beyond the fear, the pain of yesterday and learning each lesson of my past. People that I encounter can be of great value to help me as an encourager.

# DIFFICULT TIMES IN LIFE

Consider it pure joy, my brothers, and sisters, whenever you face trials of many kinds, because you know that the testing of your faith produces perseverance. Let perseverance finish its work so that you may be mature and complete, not lacking anything. (James 1:2–4)

The Bible is clear that I will experience trials. I do not know when they will come or their nature, duration, or depth, but they will come. I do know that my trials provide information to change my direction. Spiritual leaders offer me tremendous benefits as they experience trials. They help us understand God's ways and purposes in difficult times, they provide counsel and help navigate through times of crisis, and they provide comfort and stability from trusted relationships (Acts 16).

## *Prayer*

Lord, help me! I am currently in a trial. Show me your purpose and way during these difficult times. Send me a special person who will help me navigate my trial and provide me with comfort and stability.

# ESTABLISHING AND ACHIEVING GOALS

Brothers and sisters, I do not consider myself yet to have taken hold of it. But one thing I do: Forgetting what is behind and straining toward what is ahead, I press on toward the goal to win the prize for which God has called me heavenward in Christ Jesus. (Philippians 3:13–14)

My mentors provide valuable advice and constructive criticism in my personal and spiritual life. They help me think through my options and make wise choices. They monitor me and help me build trusting relationships with them and God. My mentors can suggest adjustments and counsel along the way.

The real benefit in these areas is helping ensure that the balance of my personal and spiritual goals is appropriate, e.g., keeping God as my focus and priority and ensuring that my spiritual growth is not disrupted by other pursuits. Timothy went from being a son to a student and to being a colleague and a co-laborer with Paul (1 Timothy; 2 Timothy).

## *Prayer*

Lord, keep my life balanced with your appointed mentors. Keep me focused on the right priorities so I can still grow spiritually and continue to follow your path with your purpose and plan for my life.

# TRUSTING DIRECTION
# FOR LIFE DECISIONS

Trust in the LORD with all your heart and lean not on your own understanding. In all your ways submit to him, and he will make your paths straight. (Proverbs 3:5–6)

Spiritual leaders have benefited me a lot by providing counsel in some of my major life decisions. They have given me a depth of knowledge and relationship development. Some of my life decisions came quickly, while others I was not prepared for. Regardless of the urgency, having a trusted advocate and mentor to share my major life decisions is extremely valuable.

### *Prayer*

Lord, life struggles are so difficult. Send me a trusted advocate and mentor to help me make major life decisions.

# BENEFITS OF HAVING RELATIONSHIPS IN YOUR LIFE

> Finally, brothers and sisters, whatever is true, whatever is noble, whatever is right, whatever is pure, whatever is lovely, whatever is admirable—if anything is excellent or praiseworthy—think about such things. (Philippians 4:8)

Mentors and those they mentor should listen to each other, communicate openly and without judgment, trust and respect each other, consistently make time for each other, and engage in healthy activities together.

As a mentee, I have grown in faith and pursuit of a godly, Christlike life. Virtually every other relationship I have is positively impacted. Friends, family, neighbors, coworkers, employees, and all see a changed life. This changed life has the potential to heal relationships, draw others to Christ, and influence others toward a similar experience.

## *Prayer*

Changing my life is a lifestyle that includes a change in thinking and behavior. Change me, Lord, so my relationships can be healed through my changed life. Help me to draw and influence others to a similar experience.

# A CHANGED LIFE PROVIDES OPPORTUNITIES TO GIVE BACK

"For I know the plans I have for you," declares the LORD,
"plans to prosper you and not to harm you, plans to give you
hope and a future." (Jeremiah 29:11)

Yes, changed lives have drawn me to others as I see the Spirit of God at work. He establishes the groundwork so that I potentially become a mentor to others as He leads. God's Great Commission for our lives is to make disciples. Becoming a mentor is a response to this command; the benefits to others cannot be measured in human terms but only from an eternal perspective. The true opportunity to give back and invest in the kingdom is my investing in the lives of others (Matthew 28:19).

## *Prayer*

Lord, keep me focus on the path of my purpose for you. Surrendering to your will so I may give back and invest in the kingdom and keep investing in others' lives.

# TRUTH

> Then you will know the truth, and the truth will set you free. (John 8:32)

> But when he, the Spirit of truth, comes, he will guide you into all the truth. He will not speak on his own; he will speak only what he hears, and he will tell you what is yet to come. (John 16:13)

Most often facts are true but not all truths are facts. Truth may often be used in the context of an idea of truth to self or authenticity. Due to popular culture, I could get distracted by one thing or another. Undisciplined passions from my heart could get in my way and trouble me.

Attempt first to arrange inwardly the things to be done outwardly. I try not to let my passions get the best of me but to be subject to the rulings of sound judgment. I will strive to master myself daily, grow stronger, and advance from good to better. Every day, I can be drawn closer to God, and my prayers are always for God to guide and direct my life.

## *Prayer*

Lord, continue to guide and direct my life as your Word has promised. Teach me each day you truth so that I may be the best person I can be.

# TEMPTATIONS

And lead us not into temptation but deliver us from the evil one. (Matthew 6:13)

No temptation has overtaken you except what is common to mankind. And God is faithful; he will not let you be tempted beyond what you can bear. But when you are tempted, he will also provide a way out so that you can endure it. (1 Corinthians 10:13)

On reaching the place, he said to them, "Pray that you will not fall into temptation." (Luke 22:40)

In the Bible, the word *temptation* primarily denotes a trial in which one has a free choice of being faithful or unfaithful to God; only secondarily does it signify allurement or seduction to sin. Since I have been in isolation for six months as a result of coronavirus pandemic, I have found myself faced with the challenges of boredom, loneliness, and things that could be unhealthy for me. I am high risk, but I want to work out at the gym, attend church services, surround myself with other believers, go to restaurants, listen to good music, and visit friends and family.

Currently, my life is faced with temptations, so I find myself listening to uplifting music, reading, and having long conversations with God as I take walks, sit, and read His Word several times a day.

### Prayer

Lord, deliver me from the temptations of life, and give me the courage and strength to resist the temptations in my life.

# SEASONS OF LIFE

There is a time for everything, and a season for every activity under the heavens. (Ecclesiastes 3:1)

Having been laid off and ridden with health and financial problems, I found myself having plenty of time to reflect. I find myself developing a prayer flight, examining my life, studying the Bible, volunteering in the community, and supporting others.

I am currently experiencing a dry season, a waiting-for-something season. A grinding season. A tests-and-trials-at-nearly-every-turn season, A spiritual warfare season. The list could go on. Maybe some of you are in a happy season and all is well. Sometimes, it is difficult to recognize the season of life you are in. It can be even more difficult to know how to live fully in Christ during some of the seasons.

I know that seasons change. There's winter, spring, summer, and fall. Just like the natural seasons change, so do the seasons in our lives.

It says in Ecclesiastes 3:11, "[God] has made everything beautiful in its time."

The first step to flourishing in any spiritual season is recognizing which one you are in. Which one describes your life presently?

## *Prayer*

God, you provide the seasons of life. Some are good, and some are a challenge. I need your strength and guidance during this time. Give me the courage, strength, and direction, and direct my path during the various seasons of my life.

# DRY SEASONS

Be still before the LORD and wait patiently for him; do not fret when people succeed in their ways, when they carry out their wicked schemes. (Psalm 37:7)

During a tough season, God may be quiet, and I cannot hear His voice or sense His presence as I have before. In a dry season, God appears very distant. I have lived through dry seasons, and I know how difficult they can be. For Christians, a season of spiritual dryness can be a challenge. Suddenly, their life experiences do not line up with what they know to be true about God. If God guides His children, why can't I sense it? If He cares, why don't I feel it?

I believe the key in getting through this challenging season is realizing that you are in it and pressing through it, drawing closer to God despite how far away He feels. Do not give up. Continue reading His Word. But also talk to Him even though He is quiet. Communicate with godly people you respect and admire. Because God is there. He has not left us.

## *Prayer*

God, you have been quiet during this part of my dry season, and I need guidance and direction. Please open my eyes and allow me to see the lessons of my life during this dry season.

# A SPIRITUAL DRY SPELL

*If we confess our sins, he is faithful and just and will forgive us*
*our sins and purify us from all unrighteousness. (1 John 1:9)*

Spiritual dry spells can occur after we walk through difficulties, spend time in half-heartedness or sin, or simply get stuck in a rut. In such a season, I examine my life to see if there is any issue in my heart or any unconfessed sin. If I discover it, I confess it to God and repent because dry seasons do not last forever.

In dry seasons, I keep the faith, keep trusting Him, keep going to church, and keep praising and worshipping Him even when it's hard and confusing. The rain will come.

Whether you are waiting for a godly spouse, for a difficult circumstance to change, or for God to finally fulfill a promise, your waiting season can range from mildly annoying to maddening. We know from the story of Joseph in Exodus that God leverages waiting seasons for His glory and for our good. And we know from Abraham's story in Genesis that waiting might last an awfully long time. But we also know from Hannah's story that pouring our hearts out to God and waiting on Him is totally worth it.

In your season of waiting, trust that God is pruning you of things you won't need for the next season. He is making you ready, so let Him work however long it takes.

## *Prayer*

I need help and change right now in my life. Knowing, accepting, praying, and obeying your will be done in my life give clarity of your purpose and plan for me. Lord!

# WAITING SEASONS

In the morning, LORD, you hear my voice; in the morning I
lay my requests before you and wait expectantly. (Psalm 5:3)

This season will one day be over just as all seasons will be. But times of waiting
are fairly guaranteed to happen. When I wait, I often feel I do not have enough
patience; I want to try to fix the situation my way. In such times, it is not about
learning my lesson so that I do not have to continue to wait. God wants me to
learn how to wait so I can wait well even if that implies my waiting continues
for the rest of my life.

While my plan is to keep a positive attitude and show God that I am a good
student so He will bring my waiting to a close, God wants something even better
for me. Rather than end my waiting, He wants to bless my waiting.

Even while you are waiting for God's blessing, He is ready to bless you with
the gift of Himself. Keep the faith, do not doubt God's plans and goodness, and
wait with expectancy. God is listening and knows exactly where you are. Hang
in there. God has not forgotten you.

## Prayer

Lord, this is a long season of patience. Help me focus on the hope and peace
that you give me daily and not on my past and my future but on your plans
currently for my life.

# BUSY SEASONS

In his hand are the depths of the earth, and the mountain
peaks belong to him. (Psalm 95:4)

A busy season is the "I don't have enough time to get everything done" season.
Sometimes, we have big projects or children who need more of our time than
they do in other seasons. I have just completed that season.

Busyness is becoming a value in modern American culture, but it is not
something Christians should chase. If you find yourself in a busy season, chase
after God. The key to succeeding in this time is seeking God for direction the
moment your feet hit the floor in the morning. Recognize and organize what
needs to get done, and then move through those priorities. Attacking your
priorities first will also help alleviate undue stress.

The whole world does not rest in your hands—it rests in God's hands.
Pace yourself and your tasks. Breathe. Pray. Take a lunch break. Then carry on
in your grind and press through with the strength God gives you. Rely on the
Holy Spirit to lead and help you.

## *Prayer*

Today, I almost forgot the beauty you have created. I thank you for allowing me
to take the time to see and smell my roses, see the beautiful butterflies, and the
ducks. You have allowed me to visit much of your creation and see the many
wonderful different people. Thank you for this day.

# TESTS AND TRIALS

For our light and momentary troubles are achieving for us an eternal glory that far outweighs them all. So, we fix our eyes not on what is seen, but on what is unseen, since what is seen is temporary, but what is unseen is eternal. (2 Corinthians 4:17–19)

Let us not become weary in doing good, for at the proper time we will reap a harvest if we do not give up. (Galatians 6:9)

If you are going through some hard times this season, know that God is with you during it all. He is certainly at work. It is hard for me to know this when I am in the middle of it and do not understand what I am going through or why. But I want to encourage you that God knows, and in due time, all will be revealed. In the meantime, do not give up or get tired of doing well.

If you need comfort, allow God to comfort you. If you need strength beyond yourself, let Him strengthen you. If you need wisdom, ask and the Bible promises that it will be given to you (James 1:5).

As hard as the tests and trials may be, I have allowed God to be God and to do the supernatural work only He can do. I allow Him to strengthen and increase my faith in this season of hardship or affliction.

In this season, it's essential to fix your thoughts on heavenly things, not on temporary things of this earth.

## *Prayer*

*Lord,* Thank you for the strength that you continue to give me, the peace in listening to you as I read your word, and the encouragement you provide during trials and my faith tests.

# SPIRITUAL WARFARE

> For our struggle is not against flesh and blood, but against the rulers, against the authorities, against the powers of this dark world and against the spiritual forces of evil in the heavenly realms. Therefore put on the full armor of God, so that when the day of evil comes, you may be able to stand your ground, and after you have done everything, to stand. Stand firm then, with the belt of truth buckled around your waist, with the breastplate of righteousness in place, and with your feet fitted with the readiness that comes from the gospel of peace. In addition to all this, take up the shield of faith, with which you can extinguish all the flaming arrows of the evil one. Take the helmet of salvation and the sword of the Spirit, which is the word of God. (Ephesians 6:12–17)

If you are in a season of spiritual warfare, gird up! If you are being spiritually attacked, you are doing something right that Satan does not like. If you are walking faithfully, the enemy will wage war against you. It comes with being a Christian. But do not be afraid. Remember the story of Job: God is always in complete control.

This is a wonderful thing about being God's child—He will fight for you. Just lean into Him and rely on Him by praying and reading His Word. He will take care of the rest. This is not a natural battle against flesh and blood even though it may appear to be. These are our weapons. Stand firm with the Full Armor of God proceed with the Word and Prayer.

### *Prayer*

Lord, I need help; this spiritual warfare is too much. I surrender to you. I do not have the power needed for this battle. I do know what weapons are required for me to use. Your heavenly army and all its power is ready for this battle. I surrender to you and let you take charge.

# DEATH

For God so loved the world that he gave his one and only Son, that whoever believes in him shall not perish but have eternal life. (John 3:16)

Philip said, "Lord, show us the Father and that will be enough for us." (Romans 14:8)

We humans long for life. We have an innate feeling that there is more to this world than meets the eye. It pushes us to search for our meaning in life. Those who are spiritually dead are oblivious to their state (2 Corinthians 4:4). They fail to recognize their sense of purpose are disconnected. And the fact that they are apart from God, their pursuits do not provide fulfillment.

The real danger is that without the new life that Christ gives, sinners' physical deaths will be followed by the second death (Revelation 20:14–15). Even me, a believer who leads a spiritual life, sometimes fails to fully live it by rebelling through sin. The consequence of sin is spiritual death (Romans 6:23). When believers in Christ toy with sin, they experience the deathlike symptoms of sin—a sense of distance from God.

## *Prayer*

In your word you have given me a promise about death which is about being absent from the body and to be present with you Lord. Thank you, God, for that promise.

# SPIRITUAL DEATH

> When the perishable has been clothed with the imperishable, and the mortal with immortality, then the saying that is written will come true: "Death has been swallowed up in victory." Where, O death, is your victory? Where, O death, is your sting? The sting of death is sin, and the power of sin is the law. But thanks be to God! He gives us the victory through our Lord Jesus Christ. (1 Corinthians 15:54–57)

Spiritual death is a state of being alienated from God and therefore lacking connection with Him. Believers have been given eternal life, which is summarized in John 10:10. Jesus brings us from death into life, and believers remain in life.

Spiritual death need not be a permanent state. Life awaits us. God is eager for all to come to Him (2 Peter 3:9). To be rescued from spiritual death, we need only to recognize our sinful state and call on the One who can save us.

## *Prayer*

You have given me a promise about confessing my sins and letting me now how faithful and just you are to forgive all my wrongs. Thank you.

# JUDGING

Do not judge, or you too will be judged. (Matthew 7:1)

Judging means arriving at a conclusion based on reasoning after looking at the evidence. The Bible's command that we should not judge others does not mean we cannot show discernment. Immediately after Jesus said, "Do not judge," He said, "Do not give dogs what is sacred; do not throw your pearls to pigs" (Matthew 7:6). A little later in the same sermon, He said, "Watch out for false prophets ... By their fruit you will recognize them" (Matthew 15:16). How are we to discern who are the dogs and pigs and false prophets unless we can make judgments call on doctrines and deeds?

Jesus was giving us permission to tell right from wrong. The Bible clearly teaches that truth is objective, eternal, and inseparable from God's character. Anything that contradicts the truth is a lie—but, of course, to call something a lie is to pass judgment. To call adultery or murder a sin is likewise to pass judgment—but it is also to agree with God.

When Jesus said not to judge others, He did not mean that no one could identify sin for what it is based on God's definition of sin. And the Bible's command that we do not judge others does not mean there should be no mechanism for dealing with sin. The Bible has a whole book entitled *Judges*. The judges in the Old Testament were raised up by God Himself (Judges 2:18). In saying, "Do not judge," Jesus was not saying, "Anything goes." He was not allowing injustice to continue. The modern judicial system including its judges is a necessary part of society.

### *Prayer*

Lord, Today I saw people trying to judge others and putting them down to where they had no self-confidence or self-esteem. It helps in the change process of not wanting to be judged by others. Thank you for that insight!

# JUDGING OTHERS

Do not judge, or you too will be judged. (Matthew 7:1)

You, therefore, have no excuse, you who pass judgment on
someone else, for at whatever point you judge another, you
are condemning yourself, because you who pass judgment
do the same things. (Romans 2:1)

Hypocritical judgment is wrong. Jesus gave a direct command to judge; He
told us to stop judging by appearances but instead to judge correctly. Here, we
can see a clue as to the right versus the wrong type of judgment. Taking this
verse and some others, we can put together a description of the sinful type of
judgment.

It is foolish to jump to conclusions before investigating the facts. Simon the
Pharisee passed judgment on a woman based on her appearance and reputation,
but he could not see that the woman had been forgiven; Simon then turned to
Jesus and was rebuked for his judgment (Luke 7:36–50). Unforgiving and harsh
judgment is wrong. We are always to be gentle toward everyone (Titus 3:2). The
merciful will be shown mercy (Matthew 5:7), and as Jesus warned, "In the same
way you judge others, you will be judged, and with the measure you use, it will
be measured to you" (Matthew 7:2). Self-righteous judgment is wrong. We are
called to humility, and "God opposes the proud" (James 4:6).

Untrue judgment is wrong. The Bible clearly forbids bearing false witness;
a false witness will not go unpunished, and whoever pours out lies will not go
free (Proverbs 19:5). Slander no one, be peaceable and considerate, and always
be gentle with everyone (Titus 3:2).

Christians are often accused of being judgmental or intolerant when they
speak out against sin, but opposing sin is not wrong. Holding something or
someone to standards of righteousness naturally defines unrighteousness and
draws the attention of those who choose sin over godliness. John the Baptist
spoke out against Herodias's having his brother's wife. So Herodias nursed a
grudge against John and wanted to kill him (Mark 6:18–19). Eventually, John
was silenced, but truth could not be silenced (Isaiah 40:8).

Believers are warned against judging others unfairly or righteously, but

Jesus commended "right judgment" (John 7:24). We are to be discerning (Colossians 1:9; Thessalonians 5:21). We are to preach the whole counsel of God, including the Bible's teaching on sin (Acts 20:27; 2 Timothy 4:2). We are to gently confront our brothers and sisters in Christ (Galatians 6:1). We are to practice church discipline (Matthew 18:15–17). We are to speak the truth in love (Ephesians 4:15).

## Prayer

Lord, provide me with discernment and wisdom when it comes to looking at others. Teach me to know when a person is at a teachable level and is open to learning new things and wanting changes. Help me to not allow myself to hurt other and make them feel bad about themselves.

# THE TONGUE

> Not many of you should become teachers, my fellow believers, because you know that we who teach will be judged more strictly. We all stumble in many ways. Anyone who is never at fault in what they say is perfect, able to keep their whole body in check. (James 3:1–2)

God tells us in His Word that the tongue has incredible power. We can use our tongues to bring blessings and life or curses and death. The saying "sticks and stones can break my bones, but words will never hurt me" is simply not true. Our tongues can be the most difficult thing to control, and they can leave us with great regret if we use our words to hurt.

There is hope, however. The Bible tells us that with the help of the Holy Spirit, we can have power and control over our tongues (1 Peter 3:10).

Watching our mouths and the words that come out of them is not easy. In addition to the verse above, which reminds us that our words hold the power of life and death, in Mark 11, we are reminded that our words have the power to cast entire mountains into the sea and wither fig trees.

That is why we must surrender our whole selves to Christ and remember that when we call Him Lord, it makes Him our master, and it makes us His slaves. Only with our tongues submitted to the perfect will of God can we hope to master this great power we have been given to bless Him and bless others with our loving and empowering words.

In early October 2018 and in 2020, what have been described as the deadliest forest fires in US history engulfed the dry woodlands of Northern and Southern California. As the fire raged on, the flames and intense heat killed thousands of people and consumed billions of trees. The inferno may have been started by mere sparks from utility lines or fire starters that lost control. How true are the words of James 3:5: "The tongue is a small part of the body, but it makes great boasts. Consider what a great forest is set on fire by a small spark."

The tongue is also a fire. It represents our ability to speak. Like fire, our speech has the potential to cause great harm. The Bible says that "death and life are in the power of the tongue" (Proverbs 18:21). Of course, we do not stop talking just out of concern that we might say something harmful to someone any more than we refuse to use fire because we fear the damage it might cause.

The key is control. If we control fire, we can use it to cook our food, warm our bodies, and light up dark nights. If we control our tongues, we can use their power to honor God and benefit others.

## Prayer

Lord, help me with my tongue so that I do not harm others with its power. Teach me control so I can create, uplift, and benefit others and honor you, God.

# HUMILITY

In the same way, you who are younger, submit yourselves to your elders. All of you, clothe yourselves with humility toward one another, because "God opposes the proud but shows favor to the humble." (1 Peter 5:5)

I have learned that success is all about people, teamwork, and staying humble. Nowadays, people respond to your heart. They respond to your generosity and genuine interest in them, and being humble is the key. Maybe you are just starting out, or maybe you are fully on the road to reach your goals. Either way, you will learn a lot about yourself and the importance of others on your journey through life. You will learn why humility has an impact on your entire life journey. Here are lessons you learn while reaching your goals in life.

Be humble. People will feel your heart and what's inside of it, and they will respond. Out there are countless people who have made it big and their egos have risen proportionately. But what in this life is sure? How do you know you are safe? When is the time right for you to say you have made it? I do not think there is ever a time like that. Crisis, destruction, and financial turmoil can happen at any time, and you can end up back where you started. Some of the most successful people have failed. It doesn't matter where you get or how high you reach, you should never look down on others from the top because you were once with them.

Humility will be one of the most valuable assets you can have to overcome hardships and break barriers. Never forget your beginnings or the obstacles you have overcome. Keep this in mind, and you will appreciate every person and every accomplishment.

Through the years, I engaged in useless arguments and wasted the exchange of opinions just because none of us could communicate effectively. Both minds were speaking not rationally but emotionally. It does not matter whether you are at home or at work; you will have to swallow your pride. How hard is it for you to say, "I'm sorry" or "It was my mistake"? For me, it is the toughest thing in the world, so don't feel bad. The positive news about apologies and taking responsibility it makes you mature.

Mistakes are a part of life. Everyone is guilty of making mistakes, but not knowing when to take responsibility for them is a tragedy. Pride is more of a mind game; it is not real. Pride is a perspective on yourself and who you are. If you see yourself too high, of course your pride will be much higher. How far do think you can get with a prideful mindset? There is nothing more devastating in relationships than when one side cannot admit that he or she was wrong. This situation is exactly where most relationships end. Do not let people walk over you, but do not become too difficult to communicate with. Stay humble and listen.

Sharing is caring. Any time you have an opportunity to help others, do so with all your heart because you never know when it will be your turn. Sometimes, simply go on Twitter and retweet others' posts; hit them with a comment that you loved it. They will remember you forever because you acted kindly toward them and benefited them. This is how you build relationships. This is how you can show people that you are a down-to-earth person who is on their level, who speaks their language, who is fun to interact with.

Sharing and communicating with others will be the biggest part of our journey. But to benefit from it, we must create genuine respect and care for them with all we have. We are all on the same level; we can create an amazing community around ourselves in which people love and respect us because they believe we deserve it.

## *Prayer*

Lord, teach me about choices I have made and will make. Help me to be more caring in my sharing. Allow my heart to be filled with love, caring, and compassion. Teach me daily to have humility.

# HEALING FROM YESTERDAY

The Old and New Testaments reveal that God can heal our bodies. Scriptures help us with spiritual and emotional healing. Sin, abuse, neglect, rejection, betrayal—all these cause great emotional and spiritual pain that hurts just as physical pain does. Psalms is a collection of cries, prayers, and praise.

Life lessons tend to take a life time to learn. They are the accumulated knowledge of years of living. But all life lessons are not equal. Some have more impact and greater value when we learn them earlier in life.

How do we heal from life lessons? One of the best things you can do for yourself is self-care. I set aside time to sit in silence daily even if it's just for seventy-five minutes. It sends two messages—that you care enough about yourself to make that investment, and that you are willing to listen to yourself.

Going on a silent retreat in the Colorado mountains challenged me. For the first few days, I was uncomfortable; my mind constantly wandered. But by the third day, I began to experience the power of stillness by meditating and listening to myself. It was explained as an opportunity to call my spirit back. My focus then was to have long conversations with God and read His Word.

Believing that life does not happen to you, it happens for you. Everything happens at exactly the right moment, neither too soon nor to late. That concept changed everything for me. Life is not fair. You will fail, and you will be challenged. Can you be grateful for those times that you fail or when life feels unfair? The hardest times in life make us who we are and often direct us to new, greater experiences. There's so much healing that can take place when you view every challenging experience as one that can strengthen you and guide you to where you are meant to be in your next phase of life.

Feel more, think less. The answers to some of life's hardest questions come from allowing yourself to feel. Your brain usually knows less about your needs than your heart does. Rely less on logic and more on instincts. Logic and overthinking will tell you what you are supposed to do or what looks good at surface level. Creating a calculated life that looks good on the outside will never lead to happiness, just emptiness. Learn to trust God even when doing so does not seem to make sense.

You give away your power by staying in draining situations. At what expense do you choose to stay in a draining situation? It's not just about learning to accept situations and making them work. When you choose to stay in a draining work environment or a toxic relationship, that can lead to a feeling of powerlessness. Staying in the situation requires so much energy that you are forced to give all your power away. You can protect your energy and your power by making choices that inspire you and align with your belief system.

Be vulnerable. It's beautiful! It's easy to hide behind your feelings, but it's much harder to own them, completely open your heart, and be totally vulnerable. My Yoga instructor encouraged everyone to allow themselves to be vulnerable during our time together. Being vulnerable requires strength and authenticity. The beauty is that allowing yourself to be vulnerable can lead to the most incredible connections and real-life experiences.

Bless what you do not choose, and bless what does not choose you. When you trust in the power of God, you begin to realize that what enters and exits your life is determined by God, who is larger than us all. Be grateful for the time you spend with those you do not choose and those who do not choose you. Accept that you were both meant to be on separate paths. This allows you to learn from the past and continue pursuing the life you are meant to live. Pray for the highest good for all, and trust in your own path.

### Prayer

Lord, I have learned to be open and to see the beauty that surrounds me. Thank you for helping me get through the difficult times in life.

# BE STILL

He says, "Be still, and know that I am God." (Psalm 46:10)

"Be still and know that I am God" is a popular verse for comforting ourselves and others. Many people tend to think this verse means to rest or relax in who God is. This verse does encourage believers to reflect on who God is, but there is more to this psalm.

Verse 10 is more of a wake-up call with instructions. But the command "Be still …" was written in the context of a time of trouble and war, so I have considered the verse with that context in mind. Instead of interpreting "Be still" as a gentle suggestion, the meaning in this psalm lends itself more to "Stop!" and more specifically "Stop fighting!" which is directed toward the enemies of the people of God.

The people of God should interpret the command for themselves to read more like "Snap out of it!" and "Wake up and acknowledge who God is." Verse 10 has something to say to His people: "God is our refuge and strength." The psalms are for God's people. When I realize that I am incapable of controlling life, I can only surrender my will to God's will. It may be a matter of finally saying that I trust Him. This will open the door so I can experience the fullness of God in what He has for me. God is my Creator and has a perfect plan for us when I let Him orchestrate it. "Be still and know that I am God." How can I know it is God? First, I must know that God is God, the one and only Supreme Being who created the heavens and earth (Genesis 1:1).

By practicing silence for years, I have developed time to be just with God and myself. I can know Him by having an intimate relationship with Him. That is getting to personally know Him by what He says in the Bible.

I'm telling you these things while I'm still living with you. The Friend, the Holy Spirit whom the Father will send at my request, will make everything plain to you. He will remind you of all the things I have told you. I am leaving you well and whole. That is my parting gift to you. Peace. I do not leave you the way you are used to being left—feeling abandoned. So, do not be upset. Do not be distraught. (John 14: 25–27)

When I read the Bible, I learned to recognize the way God talks to me, the kinds of things He says, and the merciful love He offers.

God is

- omniscient—all-knowing;
- omnipresent—universally present at the same time;
- omnipotent—all-powerful;
- holy, faithful, and sovereign; and
- infinite—without measure, forever.

"Be still and know that I am God; I will be honored by every nation; I will be honored throughout the world!" Some translations use the word *exalted*, which means lifted. Honored means highly valued or glorified. In this verse, we are being told that the entire world will someday lift and glorify the Lord.

## *Prayer*

Lord, help me to stop and hear you. Help me to stop fighting battles that are not mine. Teach me to surrender and turn over my internal wars and get through the difficult times in life. You are all-knowing, all-powerful, holy, faithful, and sovereign, and you are everywhere.

# SOLITUDE AND SILENCE

Be still and know that I am God. (Psalm 46:10)

Not all people are called to be hermits, but all people need enough silence and solitude in their lives to enable the deep, inner voice of their true selves to be heard occasionally. When that inner voice is not heard, when I cannot attain spiritual peace that comes from being one with my true self, I am miserable and exhausted, and my internal self will be at war. I cannot go on happily for long unless I am in contact with my spiritual life, which is hidden in the depths of my soul.

When people are evicted from homes, unemployed, facing social injustices, suffering from addictions, homeless. What happens to that person's identity? Where is their spiritual solitude? Do they continue to play a role in society?

Silence and solitude can seem out of reach of the average person who faces choices with meaning and makes differences through silence. In truth, finding solitude and silence is possible even today without having to retreat. And far from being the privilege of the few, these states are within everyone's reach. We can surrender and get through the difficult times in life with God as navigator.

## *Prayer*

Lord, teach me daily to be silent and to hear from you. Help me find my spiritual peace in learning to be one with myself and allowing you to be first in my life.

# REMORSE

Godly sorrow brings repentance that leads to salvation and leaves no regret, but worldly sorrow brings death. (2 Corinthians 7:10)

Henry admits he struggles with addiction. He is determined to beat his addiction, but he gives in and feels bad about that. He intends to make a change, but he relapses time and again, which hurts his wife. He sees the pain on her face and feels bad that he has hurt her. Henry is remorseful but not repentant. Godly sorrow produces repentance. It is based on the belief that a behavior is wrong and must be changed. It motivates one to make a behavioral change.

Regret and remorse have consequences, but they do not necessarily address the wrongdoing of those consequences. People get caught and can feel remorse because there are consequences for their actions. For example, you can speed down the highway while under the influence, get caught, and feel remorseful, but you may not feel repentant over the consequences of driving while intoxicated. You feel remorseful because you received a fine, had your license suspended, or went to jail. The conviction temporarily slows you down, but eventually, you creep back up to that speeding level and start drinking again.

## *Prayer*

Lord, I have allowed my addiction to come ahead of you. I need help in getting through the difficult times in life. I see the brokenness of my family and friends. Teach me to allow you into my life and learn to repent daily. Help me to play back the tape of the harm I created. Forgive me!

# FORGIVENESS

Jesus said, "Father, forgive them, for they do not know what they are doing." (Luke 23:34)

Forgiveness is not a feeling; it's a choice. Choosing forgiveness means going to God on your knees and surrendering to Him for the power of forgiveness. It is choosing not to let thoughts of hatred rule your heart. It is choosing to go to God to find help and comfort instead of staying in the past when you would do anything but forgive.

Forgiving people who have wronged me is one of the most difficult things God asks me to do. Cases in which Black people were killed by the police or died in their custody have risen to national prominence in recent years and have often prompted nationwide protests in some of the following cases: George Lloyd, Terence Crutcher, Philando Castile, Samuel DuBose, Sandra Bland, Freddie Gray, Walter L. Scott, Akai Gurley, Laquan McDonald, and more.

Look at the coronavirus and the losses this year in the United States. Families have had to separate and isolate. Families did not have the opportunity to be with their loved ones as they transitioned to death.

So the questions I ask are, What if the offense against me is so painful that it seems unpardonable? How can I forgive someone who broke my heart or hurt someone I loved? I have the perfect example of forgiveness in Jesus, who while in agony on the cross said in essence, "I must model my forgiveness of others on God's forgiveness of my sins." Jesus talked about the grace of forgiveness and why it was essential in the following scriptures.

If you forgive others the wrongs, they have done to you, your Father in heaven will also forgive you. But if you do not forgive others, then your Father will not forgive the wrongs you have done. (Matthew 6:14–15)

If your brother/sister sins, rebuke them, and if they repent, forgive them. If they sin against you seven times in one day, each time they come to you saying, "I repent," you must forgive them. (Luke 17:3–4)

And when you stand and pray, forgive anyone or organization you may have against anyone, so that your Father in heaven will forgive the wrongs you have done. (Mark 11:25)

Do not judge others, and God will not judge you; do not condemn others, and God will not condemn you; forgive others, and God will forgive you. (Luke 6:37)

Then Peter came to Jesus and asked, "Lord, if my brother/sister keeps on sinning against me, how many times I must forgive them? Seven times?" "No, not seven times," answered Jesus, "but seventy times seven." (Matthew 18:21–22)

Drink it, all of you; this is my blood, which seals God's covenant, my blood poured out for many for the forgiveness of sins. (Matthew 26:27–29)

## *Prayer*

Heavenly father, forgive my sins and those I have harmed in any way. For me to move on in my life and get past the struggles of my past, help me to release those I may resent and is unable to forgive. I need now to release the bondage of bitterness. Help me not to be stuck in my past.

# THANKFULNESS

Rejoice always, pray continually, give thanks in all circumstances; for this is God's will for you in Christ Jesus. (1 Thessalonians. 5:16–18)

Giving thanks in all circumstances is an attitude and action I try to follow. Thankfulness should be a way of life for us all naturally flowing from our hearts and mouths. *Thanks* is a word I use with people in nearly all situations. I say thank you to someone who passes me a glass of water and to a salesperson who brings a requested item to me. It has become a word to use when a person is courteous. But I am thankful to any act of another person who has made life more convenient and easier for me. I let others know that I appreciate their acts when I say I am thankful.

There are situations in life when a thank you just doesn't seem enough, when I am unable to express the gratitude I feel toward a person who has helped me. That is when I say I am grateful. I am grateful to God for having given me life, food, shelter, and a beautiful family, but I also feel grateful to someone who does a special favor for me. When I say or write that I am grateful, I have a deep sense of gratitude that is not reflected in a simple thank you.

Psalm 136:1 says, "Give thanks to the Lord, for he is good. His love endures forever." Here we have two reasons to be thankful: God's constant goodness and His steadfast love.

Psalm 30 gives praise to God for His deliverance. David wrote,

I will exalt you, O Lord, for you lifted me out of the depths and did not let my enemies gloat over me. O Lord my God, I called to you for help and you healed me. O Lord, you brought me up from the grave; you spared me from going down into the pit ... You turned my cries into dancing; you removed my sackcloth and clothed me with joy, that my heart may sing to you and not be silent. O Lord my God, I will give you thanks forever. (Psalm 30:1–12)

David gave thanks to God after a difficult situation. This psalm of thanksgiving praises God in the moment and remembers God's past faithfulness. It is a statement of God's character, which is so wonderful that praise is the only appropriate response.

I also have examples of being thankful during hard crises and situations. Psalm 28, for example, depicts David's distress. It is a cry to God for mercy, protection, and justice. After David cried out to God, he wrote, "Praise be to the Lord, for he has heard my cry for mercy. The Lord is my strength and my shield; my heart trusts in him, and I am helped. My heart leaps for joy and I will give thanks to him in song" (Psalm 28:6–7).

During times of hardship, David remembered who God was, and because of knowing and trusting God, he gave God thanks. Job had a similar attitude of praise even in the face of death: "The LORD gave and the LORD has taken away; may the name of the LORD be praised" (Job 1:21).

There are examples of believers' thankfulness in the New Testament as well. Paul was heavily persecuted, yet he wrote, "Thanks be to God, who always leads us in triumphal procession in Christ and through us spreads everywhere the fragrance of the knowledge of him" (2 Corinthians 2:14). The writer of Hebrews says, "Therefore, since we are receiving a kingdom that cannot be shaken, let us be thankful, and so worship God acceptably with reverence and awe" (Hebrews 12:28).

The people of God are thankful people because they realize how much they have been given. We should be thankful because God is worthy of our thanksgiving. It is only right to credit Him for "every good and perfect gift" He gives (James 1:17). When I am thankful, my focus moves off selfish desires and off the pain of current situations. Expressing thankfulness helps me remember that God is in control. Thankfulness, then, is not only appropriate; it is also healthy and beneficial. It reminds me of the bigger picture, that I belong to God, and that I have been blessed with every spiritual blessing (Ephesians 1:3). Truly, I have an abundant life (John 10:10), and gratefulness is fitting.

## Prayer

Lord, I truly thank you for life and the provisions you supply to me. You provide daily lessons in life and provide me with the gift of love in all circumstances. Thank you for getting me through the difficult times in my life. Thank you for your love and teachings. You continue to give me the strength and peace I need every day.

# ENDURANCE

Being strengthened with all power according to his glorious might so that you may have great endurance and patience. (Colossians 1:11)

I define the word *endurance* as the ability to patiently continue, to withstand hardship or adversity. It is the ability to go through and suffer without giving up in any condition and in any situation. Marathon runners set short-term goals and do not allow boredom to catch up with them.

Understanding oneself is a sure way of knowing God's purpose and plan for you. A person with a clean conscience and who leads a virtuous life and has great love and compassion can endure. The teachings of Christ illustrate that all earthy ambitions are unimportant; they stand in the way of gaining Christ. Your wisdom comes from learning God's will and making it your own.

## *Prayer*

Lord, teach me your ways and direct my path. You are transforming me into that person who continues to imitate you. Provide me with the endurance to continue with my journey. Even with the difficult times in my life my continue to be on your purpose and plan in my life. Guide my footsteps along your path with wisdom and knowledge.

# BIBLE STUDY

# TRANSFORMATION

Show me your ways, Lord, teach me your paths. Guide me
in your truth and teach me, for you are God my Savior, and
my hope is in you all day long. (Psalm 25:4–5)

## *Reflection*

_____

_____

_____

_____

_____

_____

_____

_____

_____

_____

_____

_____

_____

_____

_____

_____

_____

# TRANSFORMING INTO CHRISTLIKENESS

And we all, who with unveil faces contemplate the Lord's glory, are being transformed into his image with ever increasing glory, which comes from the Lord, who is the Spirit. (2 Corinthians 3:18)

## *Reflection*

_____

_____

_____

_____

_____

_____

_____

_____

_____

_____

_____

_____

_____

_____

_____

# STUDYING THE WORD

All Scripture is God-breathed and is useful for teaching, rebuking, correcting, and training in righteousness, So that the servant of God may be thoroughly equipped for every good work. (2 Timothy 3:16–17)

## *Reflection*

_____

_____

_____

_____

_____

_____

_____

_____

_____

_____

_____

_____

_____

_____

_____

_____

# HAVING A RENEWED MIND

Do not conform to the pattern of this world but be transformed by the renewing of your mind. Then you will be able to test and approve what God's will is—his good, pleasing, and perfect will. (Romans 12:2)

*Reflection*

_____

_____

_____

_____

_____

_____

_____

_____

_____

_____

_____

_____

_____

# THE WORD OF GOD HELPS US GET THROUGH THE DIFFICULT TIMES IN LIFE

The grass withers, the flowers fall, but the word of our God endures forever. (Isaiah 40:8)

Your word is a lamp for my feet, a light on my path. (Psalm 119:105)

Top of Form
Bottom of Form

So do not fear, for I am with you; do not be dismayed, for I am your God, I will strengthen you and help you; I will uphold you with my righteous right hand. (Isaiah 41:10)

## *Reflection*

_____

_____

_____

_____

_____

_____

_____

_____

_____

_____

# THE WORD OF GOD IS TOTALLY AUTHORITATIVE

In the beginning was the Word, and the Word was with God, and the Word was God. He was with God in the beginning. Through him all things were made; without him nothing was made that has been made. (John 1:1–3)

Top of Form
Bottom of Form

For the word of God is alive and active. Sharper than any double-edged sword, it penetrates even to dividing soul and spirit, joints, and marrow; it judges the thoughts and attitude of the heart. (Hebrews 4:12)

## *Reflection*

_____

_____

_____

_____

_____

_____

_____

_____

_____

# THE WORD OF GOD WILL ACCOMPLISH WHAT IT PROMISES

So is my word that goes out from my mouth: It will not return to me empty, but will accomplish what I desire and achieve the purpose for which I sent it. (Isaiah 55:11)

Bottom of Form

Do not conform to the pattern of this world but be transformed by the renewing of your mind. Then you will be able to test and approve what God's will is—his good, pleasing, and perfect will. (Romans 12:2)

*Reflection*

_____

_____

_____

_____

_____

_____

_____

_____

_____

_____

# HAVING A SERVANT ATTITUDE

For even the Son of Man did not come to be served, but to serve, and to give his life as a ransom for many. (Mark 10:45)

*Reflection*

_____

_____

_____

_____

_____

_____

_____

_____

_____

_____

_____

_____

_____

_____

_____

_____

# LEARNING TO BE A SERVANT

Who, being in very nature God, did not consider equality with God something to be used to his own advantage? (Philippians 2:6)

Rather, he made himself nothing by taking the very nature of a servant, being made in human likeness. (Philippians 2:7)

## *Reflection*

_____

_____

_____

_____

_____

_____

_____

_____

_____

_____

_____

_____

_____

_____

_____

# SERVANT LEADERS SACRIFICIALLY SEEK THE HIGHEST JOY OF THOSE THEY SERVE

Not so with you. Instead, whoever wants to become great among you must be your servant. (Matthew 20:26)

Just as the Son of Man did not come to be served, but to serve, and to give his life as a ransom for many. (Matthew 20: 28)

## *Reflection*

_____

_____

_____

_____

_____

_____

_____

_____

_____

_____

_____

_____

# TRAINING FOR CHANGE

I went down to the potter's house, and I saw him working at the wheel. But the pot he was shaping from the clay was marred in his hands; so, the potter formed it into another pot, shaping it as seemed best to him. Then the word of the LORD came to me. He said, "Can I not do with you, Israel, as this potter does?" declares the LORD. "Like clay in the hand of the potter, so are you in my hand, Israel." (Jeremiah 18:3–6)

## *Reflection*

_____

_____

_____

_____

_____

_____

_____

_____

_____

_____

_____

_____

_____

# BEING OPEN-MINDED

Then he opened their minds so they could understand the Scriptures. (Luke 24:45)

## *Reflection*

_____

_____

_____

_____

_____

_____

_____

_____

_____

_____

_____

_____

_____

_____

_____

_____

_____

# LEARNING FROM SPIRITUAL LEADERS

As Jesus was walking beside the Sea of Galilee, he saw two brothers, Simon called Peter and his brother Andrew. They were casting a net into the lake, for they were fishermen. "Come, follow me," Jesus said, "and I will send you out to fish for people." At once they left their nets and followed him. Going on from there, he saw two other brothers, James son of Zebedee and his brother John. They were in a boat with their father Zebedee, preparing their nets. Jesus called them, and immediately they left the boat and their father and followed him. (Matthew 4:18–22)

*Reflection*

_____

_____

_____

_____

_____

_____

_____

_____

_____

_____

_____

# SOMEONE WHO BELIEVES IN YOU

Sometime later Paul said to Barnabas, "Let us go back and visit the believers in all the towns where we preached the word of the Lord and see how they are doing." Barnabas wanted to take John, also called Mark, with them, [38] but Paul did not think it wise to take him, because he had deserted them in Pamphylia and had not continued with them in the work. They had such a sharp disagreement that they parted company. Barnabas took Mark and sailed for Cyprus, but Paul chose Silas and left, commended by the believers to the grace of the Lord. He went through Syria and Cilicia, strengthening the churches. (Acts 15:36–41)

## *Reflection*

_____

_____

_____

_____

_____

_____

_____

_____

_____

_____

# A ROLE MODEL

Follow my example, as I follow the example of Christ.
(1 Corinthians 11:1)

## *Reflection*

_____

_____

_____

_____

_____

_____

_____

_____

_____

_____

_____

_____

_____

_____

_____

_____

# PROMOTING SPIRITUAL GROWTH

Brothers and sisters, I do not consider myself yet to have taken hold of it. But one thing I do: Forgetting what is behind and straining toward what is ahead. (Philippians 3:13)

## *Reflection*

---

---

---

---

---

---

---

---

---

---

---

---

---

---

# ACCOUNTABILITY

Rooted and built up in him, strengthened in the faith as you were taught, and overflowing with thankfulness. (Colossians 2:7)

## *Reflection*

_____

_____

_____

_____

_____

_____

_____

_____

_____

_____

_____

_____

_____

_____

_____

_____

# BE AN ENCOURAGER

Joseph, a Levite from Cyprus, whom the apostles called
Barnabas (which means "son of encouragement"), [7] sold
a field he owned and brought the money and put it at the
apostles' feet. (Acts 4:36–37)

## *Reflection*

_____

_____

_____

_____

_____

_____

_____

_____

_____

_____

_____

_____

_____

_____

# DIFFICULT TIMES IN LIFE

Consider it pure joy, my brothers, and sisters, whenever you face trials of many kinds, because you know that the testing of your faith produces perseverance. Let perseverance finish its work so that you may be mature and complete, not lacking anything. (James 1:2–4)

## *Reflection*

_____

_____

_____

_____

_____

_____

_____

_____

_____

_____

_____

_____

_____

_____

_____

# ESTABLISHING AND ACHIEVING GOALS

Brothers and sisters, I do not consider myself yet to have taken hold of it. But one thing I do: Forgetting what is behind and straining toward what is ahead, I press on toward the goal to win the prize for which God has called me heavenward in Christ Jesus. (Philippians 3:13–14)

## *Reflection*

_____

_____

_____

_____

_____

_____

_____

_____

_____

_____

_____

_____

_____

_____

# TRUSTING DIRECTION
# FOR LIFE DECISIONS

Trust in the LORD with all your heart and lean not on your own understanding. In all your ways submit to him, and he will make your paths straight. (Proverb 3:5)

## *Reflection*

_____

_____

_____

_____

_____

_____

_____

_____

_____

_____

_____

_____

_____

_____

_____

_____

# BENEFITS OF HAVING RELATIONSHIPS IN YOUR LIFE

Finally, brothers and sisters, whatever is true, whatever is noble, whatever is right, whatever is pure, whatever is lovely, whatever is admirable—if anything is excellent or praiseworthy—think about such things. (Philippians 4:8)

## *Reflection*

_____

_____

_____

_____

_____

_____

_____

_____

_____

_____

_____

_____

_____

# A CHANGED LIFE PROVIDES OPPORTUNITIES TO GIVE BACK

"For I know the plans I have for you," declares the LORD, "plans to prosper you and not to harm you, plans to give you hope and a future." (Jeremiah 29:11)

## *Reflection*

_____

_____

_____

_____

_____

_____

_____

_____

_____

_____

_____

_____

_____

_____

# TRUTH

Then you will know the truth, and the truth will set you free. (John 8:32)

But when he, the Spirit of truth, comes, he will guide you into all the truth. He will not speak on his own; he will speak only what he hears, and he will tell you what is yet to come. (John 16:13)

## *Reflection*

_____

_____

_____

_____

_____

_____

_____

_____

_____

_____

_____

_____

_____

_____

# TEMPTATIONS

And lead us not into temptation but deliver us from the evil one. (Matthew 6:13)

No temptation has overtaken you except what is common to mankind. And God is faithful; he will not let you be tempted beyond what you can bear. But when you are tempted, he will also provide a way out so that you can endure it. (1 Corinthians 10:13)

On reaching the place, he said to them, "Pray that you will not fall into temptation." (Luke 22:40)

## *Reflection*

_____

_____

_____

_____

_____

_____

_____

_____

_____

_____

_____

# SEASONS OF LIFE

There is a time for everything, and a season for every activity under the heavens. (Ecclesiastes 3:1)

*Reflection*

_____

_____

_____

_____

_____

_____

_____

_____

_____

_____

_____

_____

_____

_____

_____

# DRY SEASONS

Be still before the LORD and wait patiently for him; do not fret when people succeed in their ways, when they carry out their wicked schemes. (Psalm 37:7)

## *Reflection*

_____

_____

_____

_____

_____

_____

_____

_____

_____

_____

_____

_____

_____

_____

_____

_____

_____

# A SPIRITUAL DRY SPELL

If we confess our sins, he is faithful and just and will forgive us our sins and purify us from all unrighteousness. (1 John 1:9)

## *Reflection*

_____

_____

_____

_____

_____

_____

_____

_____

_____

_____

_____

_____

_____

_____

# WAITING SEASONS

In the morning, LORD, you hear my voice; in the morning I lay my requests before you and wait expectantly. (Psalm 5:3)

## *Reflection*

_____

_____

_____

_____

_____

_____

_____

_____

_____

_____

_____

_____

_____

_____

_____

_____

_____

# BUSY SEASONS

In his hand are the depths of the earth, and the mountain peaks belong to him. (Psalm 95:4)

## *Reflection*

_____

_____

_____

_____

_____

_____

_____

_____

_____

_____

_____

_____

_____

_____

_____

_____

# TEST AND TRIALS

For our light and momentary troubles are achieving for us an eternal glory that far outweighs them all. So, we fix our eyes not on what is seen, but on what is unseen, since what is seen is temporary, but what is unseen is eternal. (2 Corinthians 4:17–19)

Let us not become weary in doing good, for at the proper time we will reap a harvest if we do not give up. (Galatians 6:9)

## *Reflection*

_____

_____

_____

_____

_____

_____

_____

_____

_____

_____

_____

_____

# SPIRITUAL WARFARE

For our struggle is not against flesh and blood, but against the rulers, against the authorities, against the powers of this dark world and against the spiritual forces of evil in the heavenly realms. Therefore put on the full armor of God, so that when the day of evil comes, you may be able to stand your ground, and after you have done everything, to stand. Stand firm then, with the belt of truth buckled around your waist, with the breastplate of righteousness in place, and with your feet fitted with the readiness that comes from the gospel of peace. In addition to all this, take up the shield of faith, with which you can extinguish all the flaming arrows of the evil one. Take the helmet of salvation and the sword of the Spirit, which is the word of God. (Ephesians 6:12–17)

*Reflection*

_____

_____

_____

_____

_____

_____

_____

_____

_____

# DEATH

For God so loved the world that he gave his one and only Son, that whoever believes in him shall not perish but have eternal life. (John 3:16)

Philip said, "Lord, show us the Father and that will be enough for us." (Romans 14:8)

## *Reflection*

_____

_____

_____

_____

_____

_____

_____

_____

_____

_____

_____

_____

_____

_____

_____

_____

# SPIRITUAL DEATH

When the perishable has been clothed with the imperishable, and the mortal with immortality, then the saying that is written will come true: "Death has been swallowed up in victory." "Where, O death, is your victory? Where, O death, is your sting?" The sting of death is sin, and the power of sin is the law. But thanks be to God! He gives us the victory through our Lord Jesus Christ. (1 Corinthians 15:54–57)

## *Reflection*

_____

_____

_____

_____

_____

_____

_____

_____

_____

_____

_____

_____

_____

_____

# JUDGING

Do not judge, or you too will be judged. (Matthew 7:1)

## *Reflection*

_____

_____

_____

_____

_____

_____

_____

_____

_____

_____

_____

_____

_____

_____

_____

_____

_____

_____

# JUDGING OTHERS

Do not judge, or you too will be judged. (Matthew 7:1)

You, therefore, have no excuse, you who pass judgment on someone else, for at whatever point you judge another, you are condemning yourself, because you who pass judgment do the same things. (Romans 2:1)

## *Reflection*

_____

_____

_____

_____

_____

_____

_____

_____

_____

_____

_____

_____

# THE TONGUE

How could we ever hope to tame such a thing as the tongue?

Not many of you should become teachers, my fellow believers, because you know that we who teach will be judged more strictly. We all stumble in many ways. Anyone who is never at fault in what they say is perfect, able to keep their whole body in check. (James 3:1–2)

## *Reflection*

_____

_____

_____

_____

_____

_____

_____

_____

_____

_____

_____

_____

_____

_____

_____

# HUMILITY

In the same way, you who are younger, submit yourselves to your elders. All of you, clothe yourselves with humility toward one another, because, "God opposes the proud but shows favor to the humble."

## *Reflection*

_____

_____

_____

_____

_____

_____

_____

_____

_____

_____

_____

_____

_____

_____

_____

# HEALING FROM YESTERDAY

Getting through difficult times in life we do not give in and we do not give up because with time everything will be alright.

## *Reflection*

_____

_____

_____

_____

_____

_____

_____

_____

_____

_____

_____

_____

_____

_____

_____

# BE STILL

He says, "Be still, and know that I am God." (Psalm 46:10)

## *Reflection*

_____

_____

_____

_____

_____

_____

_____

_____

_____

_____

_____

_____

_____

_____

_____

_____

# SOLITUDE AND SILENCE

He says, "Be still, and know that I am God." (Psalm 46:10)

## *Reflection*

_____

_____

_____

_____

_____

_____

_____

_____

_____

_____

_____

_____

_____

_____

_____

_____

_____

# REMORSE

Godly sorrow brings repentance that leads to salvation and leaves no regret, but worldly sorrow brings death. (2 Corinthians 7:10)

## *Reflection*

_____

_____

_____

_____

_____

_____

_____

_____

_____

_____

_____

_____

_____

_____

# FORGIVENESS

Jesus said, "Father, forgive them, for they do not know what they are doing." (Luke 23:34)

## *Reflection*

_____

_____

_____

_____

_____

_____

_____

_____

_____

_____

_____

_____

_____

_____

_____

_____

_____

_____

# THANKFULNESS

Rejoice always, pray continually, give thanks in all circumstances; for this is God's will for you in Christ Jesus. (1 Thessalonians 5:16–18)

## *Reflection*

_____

_____

_____

_____

_____

_____

_____

_____

_____

_____

_____

_____

_____

# LOVING

Whoever does not love does not know God, because God is love. (1 John 4:8)

Greater love has no one than this: to lay down one's life for one's friends. (John 15:13)

## *Reflection*

_____

_____

_____

_____

_____

_____

_____

_____

_____

_____

_____

_____

_____

_____

_____

_____

# TEACH ME TO LOVE UNCONDITIONALLY

But I tell you, love your enemies and pray for those who persecute you, that you may be children of your Father in heaven. He causes his sun to rise on the evil and the good and sends rain on the righteous and the unrighteous. (Matthew 5:44–45)

## *Reflection*

_____

_____

_____

_____

_____

_____

_____

_____

_____

_____

_____

_____

_____

_____

# WHAT IS GODLY LOVE?

Whoever claims to love God yet hates a brother or sister is a liar. For whoever does not love their brother and sister, whom they have seen, cannot love God, whom they have not seen. 21 And he has given us this command: Anyone who loves God must also love their brother and sister. (1 John 4:20–21)

## *Reflection*

_____

_____

_____

_____

_____

_____

_____

_____

_____

_____

_____

_____

_____

_____

# NO EXCEPTIONS TO LOVE

If I give all I possess to the poor and give over my body
to hardship that I may boast, but do not have love, I gain
nothing. Love is patient, love is kind. It does not envy, it does
not boast, it is not proud. It does not dishonor others, it is
not self-seeking, it is not easily angered, it keeps no record
of wrongs. Love does not delight in evil but rejoices with the
truth. It always protects, always trusts, always hopes, always
perseveres. (1 Corinthians 13:3–7)

## *Reflection*

_____

_____

_____

_____

_____

_____

_____

_____

_____

_____

_____

_____

# GIFT OF GIVING

Joseph, a Levite from Cyprus, whom the apostles called
Barnabas (which means "son of encouragement"), sold a
field he owned and brought the money and put it at the
apostles' feet. (Acts 4:36–37)

## *Reflection*

_____

_____

_____

_____

_____

_____

_____

_____

_____

_____

_____

_____

_____

_____

# ENDURANCE

Being strengthened with all power according to his glorious
might so that you may have great endurance and patience.
(Colossians 1:11)

## *Reflection*

_____

_____

_____

_____

_____

_____

_____

_____

_____

_____

_____

_____

_____

_____

# SUBJECT TITLES (ALPHABETICAL)

Accountability
A Changed Life Provides Opportunities to Give Back
A Spiritual Dry Spell
A Renewed Mind
A Role Model
A Servant Attitude
*Servant Leaders Sacrificially Seek the Highest Joy of Those They Serve
Be Still
Be an Encourager
Being Open-Minded
Benefits of Having Relationships in Your Life
Busy Seasons
In Times of Crisis
Death
Difficult Times in Life
Dry Season
Endurance
Establishing and Achieving Goals
Feel More, Think Less
Forgiveness
Gift of Giving
Godly Love
Having a Renewed Mind
Healing from Life Lessons
Humility
Judging
Judging Others
Learning from Spiritual Leaders
Learning to Be a Servant
Loving
No Exceptions to Love
Promoting Spiritual Growth

Remorse
Seasons of Life
Solitude and Silence
Someone Who Believes in You
Spiritual Warfare
Spiritual Death
Studying the Word
Temptations
Tests and Trials
Thankfulness
The Tongue
Trusting Direction for Life Decisions
The Word of God Is Totally Authoritative
The Word Speaks to Us during Difficult Times in Life
The Word of God Will Accomplish What It Promises
Training for Change
Transformation
Transforming into Christlikeness
Truth
Waiting Seasons
What Is Godly Love?

Dear Readers,

I named this book *Getting through the Difficult Times in Life* because our pasts are often full of hurt and disappointments, whether it is a dysfunctional childhood, a divorce, a death of a loved one, or the loss of a business, a career, or even relocation to a different geographical area. Leaving family and friends behind can bring a lot of sadness. This can leave us feeling as if we have no power to change. We may view it as being a part of our lives as being stuck or finished.

We must move to a different chapter of our lives and learn from life's lessons. If we get stuck in our past, we are unable to move forward. A part of our lives is gone, is over, and we must grieve the loss of our old lives. Looking at new beginnings means that we must change. I wonder how some people can move quickly through their lives and step into new beginnings so frequently.

Our journey in life is important and full of lessons. We must recognize periods when change is needed and that new beginnings every day are full of gifts from God. *Getting through the Difficult Times in Life* helped me learn that my past is full of people, events, and situations that I failed to grieve about. I hope this book will help those who may be stuck in the past or are in situations and may be fearful of moving forward.

God transforms us and uses us for a purpose in life to help others and expand His kingdom. This book is meant for readers who are sixteen years and older. It is for those at all stages of their spiritual development and their life journeys, regardless of whether they are new or mature believers. A wide variety of experiences with views, concepts, and challenges has been provided. I hope the topics will help everyone in what he or she needs at any given time.

## *Prayer*

May you find peace and allow God to help you get through the difficult times in life to transform your yesterday into new beginnings of today.

# VISION BOARD INSTRUCTIONS

As you experience difficult times, a vision board is a wonderful tool to reflect on your attitudes and beliefs and create events, circumstances, and opportunities to live out those attitudes and beliefs. A vision board is a tool for turning your greatest dreams into reality. It will provide hope through your difficult times. It will help you narrow down your desires and the choices you make as well as invest time and energy to visualize your future and remind you of your life goals.

## Choice

Identify your wishes or desires and select images that represent them. You might decide to put a picture of a house on your vision board because you want to purchase your dream home one day. There is power in focusing on the details of how to represent your desire. Making your choices sends a specific and personalized message to God about your desires. Maybe a picture of a university reflects your desire to seek higher education. Remember that your images must represent your specific desire—whether you want to become an attorney, doctor, or engineer, or perhaps a nurse or accountant. Send a specific and personalized message to God.

## Visualization

By repeatedly visualizing an event, situation, object, or person, you command your subconscious mind that this is what you want and this is what it must seek. There is no magic to visualization. It's nature's process of using thought power to imprint a desire and a command into the mind and then project the right kind of energetic vibration that will attract what you desire.

## Consistency

Consistency is the key to learning new skills or making changes in your life. By creating a vision board and placing it in a spot you see every day, you create the opportunity for consistent visualization to train your mind, body, and spirit to manifest your desire. The wonderful thing about your vision board is that it requires time and energy for your creation.

## Planning Your Vision Board

Thoughtfully consider the message you want your personalized board to convey and how you want it to look.

What wishes and desires do you want to reflect on your dream board? Think about these.

- your values
- family life
- love life
- health and wellness
- self-care

What do you want to learn or grow into? Do you want one board or multiple boards for different areas of your life? Maybe you prefer making several small boards to visualize several categories of desires, or you may prefer one large board that encompasses all your desires. You can source these images from a variety of places.

- newspaper cutouts
- magazine cutouts
- images of quotes printed from the internet
- photographs
- pages from a book
- brochures/pamphlets/flyers

Images are a major component of a vision board. Use stick glue tape or hot glue for precious items or photographs; buy acid-free, removable adhesive that is safe for photos.

- Find a quiet space.
- Set out all your supplies.
- Light some candles or incense.
- Turn on some music.
- Meditate or say a prayer before you begin.

Once you have created your vision board, place it in an area that you see every day. Your vision will then become a positive motivator to enact on achieving your goals.